SEWING

17 New Designs from Helen Philipps,
Exploring Her Love of Fabrics, Patchwork and Colour

HELEN PHILIPPS

Tuva Publishing

www.tuvapublishing.com

Address Merkez Mah. Cavusbasi Cad. No71
Cekmekoy - Istanbul 34782 / Turkey
Tel +9 0216 642 62 62

Home Sweet Home Sewing

First Print 2020 / August

All Global Copyrights Belong To
Tuva Tekstil ve Yayıncılık Ltd.

Content Sewing

Editor in Chief Ayhan DEMİRPEHLİVAN
Project Editor Kader DEMİRPEHLİVAN
Author Helen PHILIPPS
Technical Editors Leyla ARAS, Büşra ESER
Graphic Designers Ömer ALP
Abdullah BAYRAKÇI, Tarık TOKGÖZ
Photography Tuva Publishing, Helen PHILIPPS
Illustrations Murat Tanhu YILMAZ

ISBN 978-605-7834-08-9

f TuvaYayincilik @ TuvaPublishing
t TuvaYayincilik @ TuvaPublishing

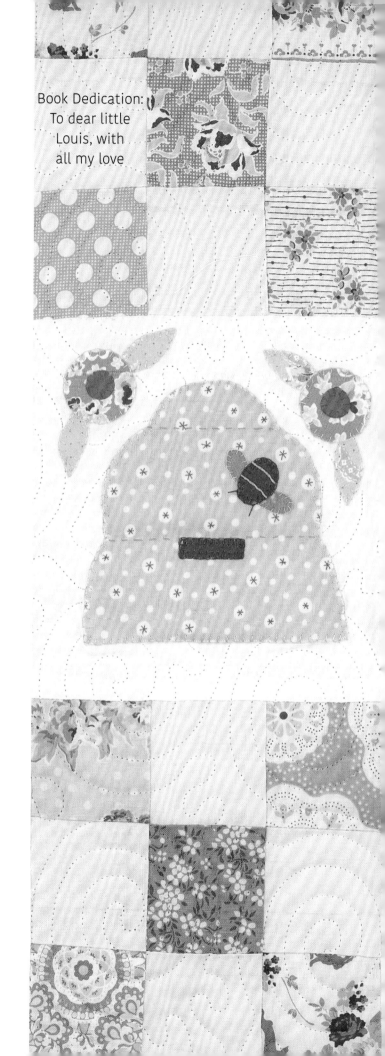

Book Dedication:
To dear little
Louis, with
all my love

CONTENTS

PROJECTS

INTRODUCTION

Home Sweet Home Sewing is a collection of sweet and fresh new projects inspired by the traditional crafts of patchwork, quilting and embroidery but with a contemporary twist which makes them fit well in modern interiors.

I have explored my love of fabrics here too, and show ways to use up even the tiniest scraps. I love to use a special fabric colour palette to create the different projects, from soft and romantic to bright and fresh, and exploring colour is a way to make each project your own. I learnt how to do patchwork using the English paper piecing technique when I was a school girl. I love to sew by hand still, but I also appreciate the speed of machine sewing and chain piecing and I have included projects for all these in my new book.

The selection of projects includes the soft and floral Honey Hives Quilt and the cute Little Houses Quilt, as well as the very sweet Little Birds Doll's Quilt that includes simple embroidery. There are lots of smaller makes like patchwork cushions, including the Liberty Circles Cushion that uses up tiny precious scraps of fabric, the pretty pastel Spring Wreath, cute Little Deer toy, handstitched pincushions and other sewing notions, table topper, pretty fabric bags, coasters, charms and decorations. Many of these simple patterns provide a good starting point to explore your own creativity, and I hope they will inspire you to create and have a lot of crafty fun.

Happy sewing!

Helen

PROJECT GALLERY

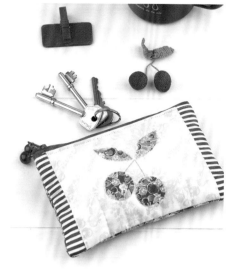

P.10

P.14

P.20

P.24

P.28

P.34

P.38

P.44

P.48

P.52

P.56

P.60

P.64

P.68

P.72

P.76

P.82

PROJECTS

cherry
ZIPPER POUCH

Small zipper pouches are a favourite sewing project because they are quick and fun to make and also very useful. This pattern can be made up in so many different fabrics and colours that the options are endless. This little cherry pouch is appliqued and quilted and the red zipper forms part of the design.. Finished off with a cute little cherry zipper pull.

Size
6 ¼ in x 4 in (16 x 10 cm) approx

11

YOU WILL NEED

- Light coloured fabric 5 ¾ in x 4 ½ in (14.61 x 11.43cm)
- Red and white striped fabric – 2 strips 1 ¼ in x 4 ½ in (3.17 x 11.43cm)
- Scraps of red and green fabric
- Fusible web
- Grey sewing cotton
- Dark grey embroidery thread
- Backing fabric 7 ½ in x 4 ½ in (19.05 x 11.43cm)
- 2 pieces of batting 7 ½ in x 4 ½ in (19.05 x 11.43cm)
- 2 pieces of lining fabric each 7 ½ in x 4 ½ in (19.05 x 11.43cm)
- Zipper 7 ½ in (19.05) - trim to fit
- Thin card for templates
- Frixion pen

1 Trace the cherry and leaf shape onto thin card and cut out to make the templates.

2 Take a scrap of red fabric and iron fusible web onto the back. Do the same with a piece of green fabric. Place the cherry template onto the back of the red fabric and draw round it twice. Place the leaf template onto the back of the green fabric and draw round it twice. Cut out the cherries and the leaves.

3 Take the piece of light coloured fabric for the pouch front and sew the strips of red and white striped fabric at both side edges with a ¼ in (6mm) seam. Press.

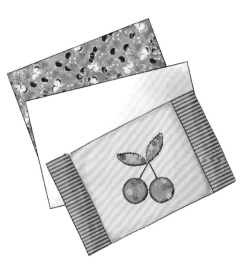

4 Arrange the cherries and leaves on the front of the pouch and then peel off the paper backing and iron them in place. Sew round the applique shapes using pale grey cotton and blanket stitch.

5 Draw the line for the stems with a Frixion then stitch it using couching stitch.

6 Press the front of the pouch, and layer ready for quilting by first placing a lining piece face down on a flat surface, then a piece of wadding on top and then the front of the pouch on top facing upwards. Use curved basting pins to hold the layers in place.

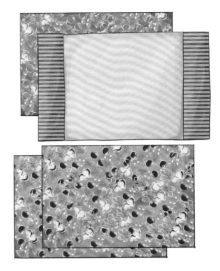

7 Quilt around the cherries and leaves, and quilt a couple of horizontal lines right across the front of the pouch. You can do as much or as little quilting as you wish.

8 Take the backing piece and prepare for quilting in the same way, then quilt horizontal lines across it as on the front.

9 To sew the zipper in place take the front of the pouch and with right side facing line up the zipper along the top edge, pin and then baste in place. Stitch along the zipper close to the edge if you would like the colour of the zipper to show as part of the design. Top stitch along the front of the pouch close to the edge. Repeat the process with the second side of the zipper and the back of the pouch.

10 OPEN the zipper now and place the back and the front of the pouch right sides together, aligning them at the sides and the bottom. Sew right round the pouch with a ¼ in (6mm) seam. Trim the edges neatly and clip the corners. You can use pinking shears or stitch a zig zag stitch to finish off the seams if you wish.

11 Turn the pouch out to the right side and push the corners out carefully.

12 Add a tiny cherry charm to the zipper pull if you wish.

dresden PINCUSHION

This pretty little pincushion is based on a traditional Dresden Plate quilt block, using English paper pieced patchwork and needle turn applique. It is a good project to start with if you would like to try these techniques. The fresh colours and floral fabrics bring a summer feeling to your sewing all year round. You can play around with other fabrics and colours to create your own pretty Dresden pincushion.

Size
4 in x 4 in (10.16 x 10.16 cm)

YOU WILL NEED

- One square of pink striped fabric
  4 ½ in x 4 ½ in (11.5 x 11.5cm)

- One square of white floral fabric
  4 ½ in x 4 ½ in (11.5 x 11.5cm)

- Scraps of red and white spotted
  fabric and blue floral for Dresden
  flower

- Four strips of red and blue printed
  fabric 4 ½ in x 1 ½ in (11.5 x 3.8cm)
  for sides

- Covered button to match

- Small flower button

- Thin card

- Scrap paper

- Glue pen

1 Trace the Dresden paper piece shape onto thin card and cut out.

2 Draw round the shape onto scrap paper ten times to make ten petals.

3 From red and white spotted fabric cut out five petals slightly bigger all the way round than the petal template. Cut five shapes in the same way from the blue floral fabric.

4 Take the paper pieces and cover each one carefully with fabric using the glue pen sparingly at the edges to secure in place.

5 Place the petals in a circle alternating the blue and the white. Place a blue petal and a white petal right sides together and sew them with tiny over stitches along one edge. When all the petals are sew together remove the papers and press, still keeping the edges turned under.

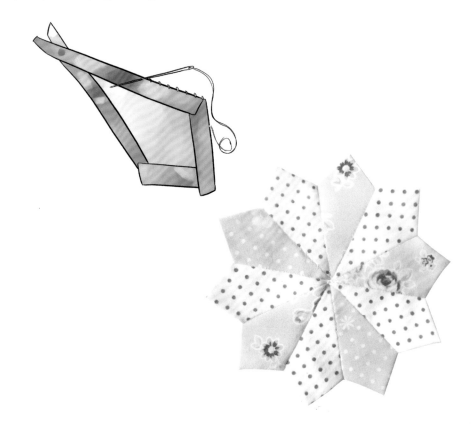

1 Press the pincushion top and place the Dresden flower in the centre. Use tiny applique pins to hold in place. Sew the Dresden flower to the backing using tiny stitches and the needle turn applique technique.

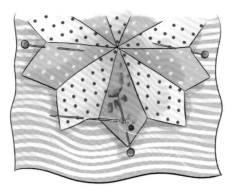

2 Take the four sides of the pincushion and arrange them round the top till you are happy with the layout. Join the long strips together at the short ends, joining the final seam to form a loop.

3 Pin the fabric loop round the pincushion top, right sides together and matching the corners, then sew with a ¼ in (6mm) seam all the way round.

4 Take the white floral backing square and pin and sew the pincushion sides to it in the same way, right sides together and leaving a small gap for turning.

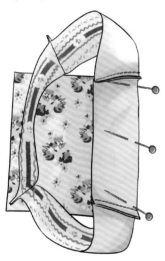

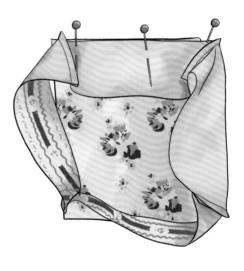

5 Turn the pincushion the right way out and press the seams and corners. Stuff firmly with polyester toy filling and sew the gap closed neatly.

6 Finally sew on the covered button in the centre of the Dresden flower, sewing through the smaller button in the centre of the back at the same time.

flower
BAG

This small tote bag would make a lovely thank you gift for a special person, filled with sweets, crafts items or a new book perhaps. The soft striped fabric bag is lined with a pretty polka dot print and has wonderful readymade cherry handles which are very easy to attach. The little flower with its covered button centre makes a cute decoration. You could add more flowers or other embellishments too if you liked or keep it smart and simple.

Finished Size
8in x 8in (20.32 x 20.32 cm) approx. (excluding handles)

YOU WILL NEED

- 2 pieces pink and white striped furnishing weight fabric for front and back each 10in x 9in (25.4 x 22.86 cm)

- 2 pieces spotty pink and white fabric for lining 10in x 9in (25.4 x 22.86 cm)

- Purchased cherry handles

- Pink and white spotty flower (made from the Fabric Flower pattern also used for the Spring Wreath)

- Covered button for flower centre

1 Place the front and back pieces of the bag right sides together and sew round the sides and bottom seams with a ¼ in (6mm) seam.

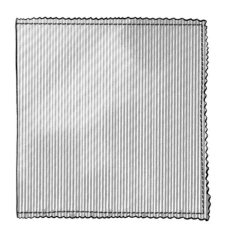

2 Clip the corners and trim the seams.

3 Box the corners by making a 1½ in (3.81cm) mark, match up the side and bottom seams then draw a straight line at the mark and sew across. Do the same on the other side of the bag.

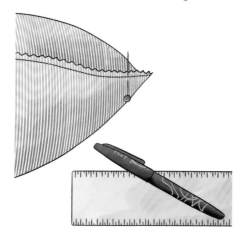

4 Take the two lining fabric pieces and sew in the same way but leaving a small gap in the bottom of the lining for turning. Box the corners of the lining in the same way as you did for the main part of the bag.

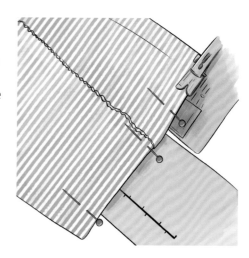

5 Place the lining and the bag right sides together and sew round the top. Pull the bag through the gap in the lining and smooth out. Sew up the gap in the lining and push it neatly inside the bag. Using matching cotton top stitch around the top edge. Press.

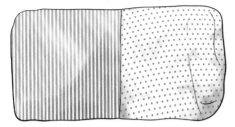

6 Attach the purchased cherry handles according to the manufacturer's instructions.

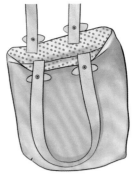

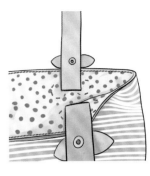

7 To finish make a fabric flower from pink and white spotty fabric following the instructions below.

Make a Flower

1 Trace the circle template onto thin card and cut out carefully.

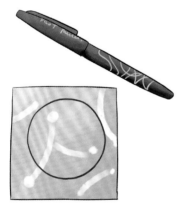

3 Fold one circle in half and sew round the raw edge with white cotton and running stitch, pulling it up to gather. Go straight on to the next petal in the same way. When all five petals are joined pull the thread to gather them all up, place the first and last petals together and overstitch to finish. Glue a small circle of white felt onto the back of the flower to secure the petals.

2 Place the circle onto the back of the pink fabric and draw round it five times to make five petals.

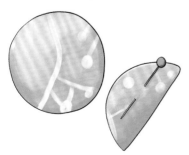

4 To make a covered button you will need a circle of green floral fabric and a button shell. Sew a line of running stitch round the outside of the circle and pull up round the button shell. Over sew at the back to secure. Push the round button back into place to finish. Glue the covered button to the centre of the pink flower with a glue gun or strong glue.

5 Make another two pink flowers in the same way.

flower CONE

This is such a simple idea but using different fabrics and trims can make it extra special. The little fabric cone looks very pretty filled with faux flowers to brighten up a corner, and it would also make a lovely gift filled with sweets or other small treats. You could make a set of them to hang in a row too to celebrate a birthday or wedding anniversary.

Size
5 ½ in x 6 ½ in (13.97 x 16.51cm) approx

YOU WILL NEED

- Pink check fabric 8in x 8in (20.32 x 20.32cm)

- Grey floral fabric 8in x 8in (20.32 x 20.32cm)

- Wadding 8in x 8in (20.32 x 20.32cm)

- Thin card

- Decorative ribbon

- Tiny button

- Twine or ribbon to hang

1 Trace the cone shape onto thin card and cut out to make the template.

2 Take the pink check fabric, fold it in half right sides together and place the template with one long edge along the fold. Draw round the shape and cut it out. This will be the lining.

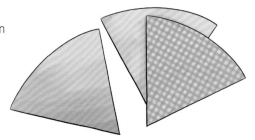

3 Fold the grey floral fabric in half and repeat the process for the outside of the cone.

4 Fold the wadding in half, place the template on the fold and cut round it.

5 Take the outer fabric and lining fabric and place right sides together, then place the wadding on top of the lining. Using a ¼ in (6mm) seam sew round the top curved edge.

6 Pull open the cone shape so the seam is across the middle and place right sides together long ways.

7 Sew along the long edge leaving an opening in the lining seam. Turn the cone right side out, pushing out the points. Sew up the gap neatly and push the lining inside the outside part of the cone. Topstitch close to the top edge.

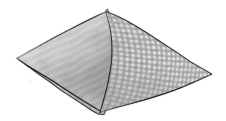

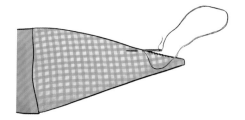

8 Sew some decorative ribbon around the top of the cone, add a little button and some ribbon for hanging. Fill with faux flowers and hang.

needle book
AND
Scissor Keep

This cute little set of needle book and scissor keep is easy to sew, fun to make - and very useful too. You can use any fabrics you like and add buttons and ribbons to personalise your design. The sweet little scissor keep means your scissors will always be to hand. It couldn't be easier to make and is a great way to use up the tiniest of scraps.

Size
3 ¼ in x 3 ¾ in (8.26 x 9.53cm) approx

YOU WILL NEED

- Red and cream print fabric for front 3 ½ in x 4 ½ in (8.89 x 11.43cm)

- Light print fabric for back 3 ½ in x 4 ½ in (8.89 x 11.43cm)

- Red and white striped fabric 1 ½ in x 4 ½ in (3.81 x 11.43cm) for spine

- Red and white striped fabric scrap for heart applique

- Wadding 7 ½ in x 4 ½ in (19.05 x 11.43cm)

- Striped backing fabric 7 ½ in x 4 ½ in (19.05 x 11.43cm)

- 2 felt pages pale pink 6in x 3 ½ in (15.24 x 8.89cm)

- Red and white ribbon 15in (38cm)

- Scraps of red white and green fabric for applique

- Thin card

- Fusible web

1 Place the red and cream fabric front and the red and white striped spine fabric right sides together and sew along the long edge with a ¼ in (6mm) seam. Sew the back piece of the needle book to the other side of the spine in the same way.

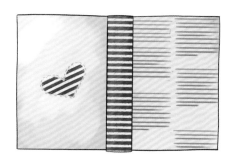

2 Trace the flower pot, the leaf, the flower circles and the heart shape onto thin card and cut out to make the templates.

3 Iron fusible web onto the back of scraps of green, red and white fabrics for the flower pot applique and onto red and white striped fabric for the heart applique.

4 Draw round the flower pot shape onto the back of the red fabric and cut out. Place on the front of the needle book and iron on, then sew round it with blanket stitch and matching cotton. Draw round the leaf onto the back of the green fabric and round the large circles on the red fabric. Draw round the smaller circle on the back of the white fabric. Cut out the flowers and the leaf, place them on the front of the needle book as in the photo and iron them in place. Sew round the edges with blanket stitch and matching cotton. Use green embroidery cotton to couch stitch a stem for each flower.

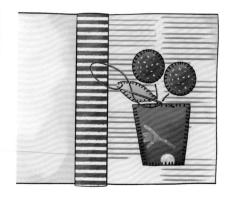

5 Take the scrap of red and white striped cotton and iron fusible web on the back. Draw round the heart shape and cut it out. Place it on the back of the needle book and iron it on. Sew round it with blanket stitch and matching cotton. Sew a line of running stitch round the heart with red cotton.

6 Place a piece of thin wadding behind the needle book and quilt round the applique shapes and along the spine.

7 Cut the red and white ribbon in half. Place the needle book right sides together with the lining fabric and insert the ribbon to the front and back edges so it will be sewn into the lining, pinning in place. Sew round the needle book leaving a small gap for turning. Trim the seams and clip the corners, turn the needle book the right way out, carefully pushing out the corners, and press. Top stitch round the whole needle book, closing the gap left for turning as you do so.

8 Fold the pale pink felt pages in half and place them in the centre of the needle book. Sew down the centre of the spine and the centre of the felt pages, pinning to keep in place while you sew.

9 Finally tie the ribbons in a bow to finish. .

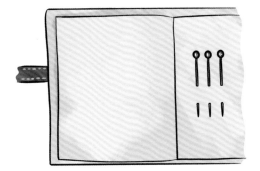

Scissor Keep

YOU WILL NEED

- Red and cream fabric 2 ½ in square (6.35cm)

- White spotted fabric 2 ½ in square (6.35cm)

- Red and white baker's twine 10 ½ in (26.67cm)

- Polyester toy filling

- Red wooden heart button

- Small round red button

1 Place the two squares of fabric right sides together, with the baker's twine pinned into one corner so it will be sewn into the seam.

2 Sew around the square leaving a small gap for turning. Clip the corners and turn the scissor keep the right way out, pushing out the corners. Stuff with a small amount of polyester toy filling and sew the gap closed.

3 Sew a red wooden heart button to the centre of the front and a small round red button to the centre of the back.

hexagon
FLOWER COASTER

Hexagons are a traditional patchwork shape and are always
a pleasure to sew and to use. This little project uses hexagons to form
the classic flower block to make a neat little set of coasters, quilted
and backed with felt. They would make a sweet little gift and you
could choose any fabrics to make your own matching set.

Size
4 1/2 in (11.43cm) wide

YOU WILL NEED

- Selection of floral fabrics in reds, teal and cream

- Fusible wadding

- Thin card

- Scrap paper

- Glue pen

- Light grey sewing cotton

- Soft cream cotton 16in (40.5cm)

1 Trace the hexagon template onto thin card and cut out. Take a piece of scrap paper and draw round the hexagon template onto it seven times then cut out the paper hexagons.

2 From floral fabrics cut one cream hexagon shape and five red hexagon shapes a little bigger all round than the template. Take one paper piece hexagon and one fabric hexagon and fold the hexagon fabric neatly round the paper piece, using the glue pen sparingly and folding over one side at a time.

3 Sew the red hexagons to the centre cream hexagon and join the remaining seams until you have a flower shape.

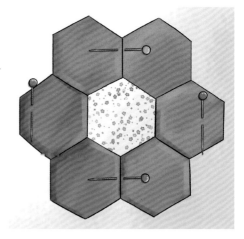

4 Remove the paper pieces and press the edges of the hexagon flower inwards as if the papers were still in place.

5 Take the backing fusible wadding and lay the hexagon flower on top (do not cut it out until you have sewn it) then top sew along the edges all the way round, and stitch in the ditch along the hexagon shapes.

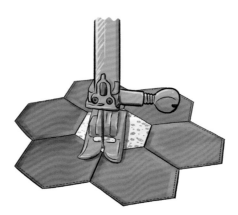

Cut away the wadding close to the edge of the hexagon shape.

6 Make four more hexagon coasters in the same way, and then stack them up together and tie a bow around them with soft cream cotton.

honey hives
QUILT

This beautiful quilt was inspired by English country gardens, buzzing bees and old fashioned beehives amongst pretty flowers and soft foliage. The quilt features just two repeating blocks, a simple nine patch and an applique beehive block. It uses lots of subtle colours for the fabrics in the nine patch blocks and simple fusible web applique for the hives and bees blocks. It is a sweet quilt to remind us of summer gardens all year round.

Size
33 ½ in x 39 ½ in (85.09 x 100.33cm) approx

YOU WILL NEED

- White cotton solid fabric 1 yd (0.91m)
- Pale pink cotton solid fabric 1yd (0.91m)
- Beige print 1yd (0.91m)
- Scraps for flowers - pink floral, green floral, deep pink
- Tilda scraps - florals in pinks, greens, grey for 75 2 ½ in (6.35cm) squares
- Yellow embroidery thread
- Fusible web
- Embroidery cotton to match the appliques
- Thin card for templates
- Border fabric 1 yd (91.44 cm)
- Batting 1 ½ yd (137.16cm)
- Backing fabric 1 ½ yd (137.16cm)
- Striped binding fabric ½ yd (45.72cm)

1 Trace the beehive shape, the bee body and wing shapes and the pink flowers and leaf shapes onto thin card and cut out carefully.

2 Cut a 6 ½ in (16.51cm) square of white solid fabric.

3 Take a 5in (12.7cm) square of beige printed fabric and iron fusible web onto the back. Place the beehive template on the back and draw round it. Cut out the beehive.

4 Take the solid white square and fold it in half and in half again to find the centre. Fold the beehive in the same way and then remove the paper backing and position it in the centre of the white square. Align the creases, then iron the beehive in place. Sew round the beehive shape using matching cotton and blanket stitch.

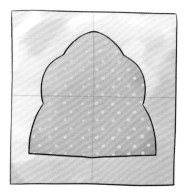

5 Take a piece of dark grey cotton fabric and iron fusible web on the back. Place the bee body shape template on the back and draw round it. Also place the beehive door shape on it and draw round that too.

6 Take a piece of pale grey fabric and iron fusible web on the back, and draw round the bee wing shape onto it twice. Cut out the bee body and wings, and the beehive door shape. Follow the diagram and photo to see how to place the bee and the door. Iron them in place and sew round the shapes with matching cotton.

7 Finish the bee by embroidering two sets of long stitches in yellow embroidery thread across the back, couching them down.

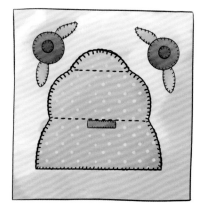

8 For the flowers draw round the large and small circles onto thin card and cut them out carefully. Draw round the leaf shape and cut it out too. Iron fusible web onto the back of pink floral fabric, solid pink fabric and green fabric.

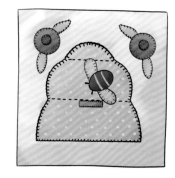

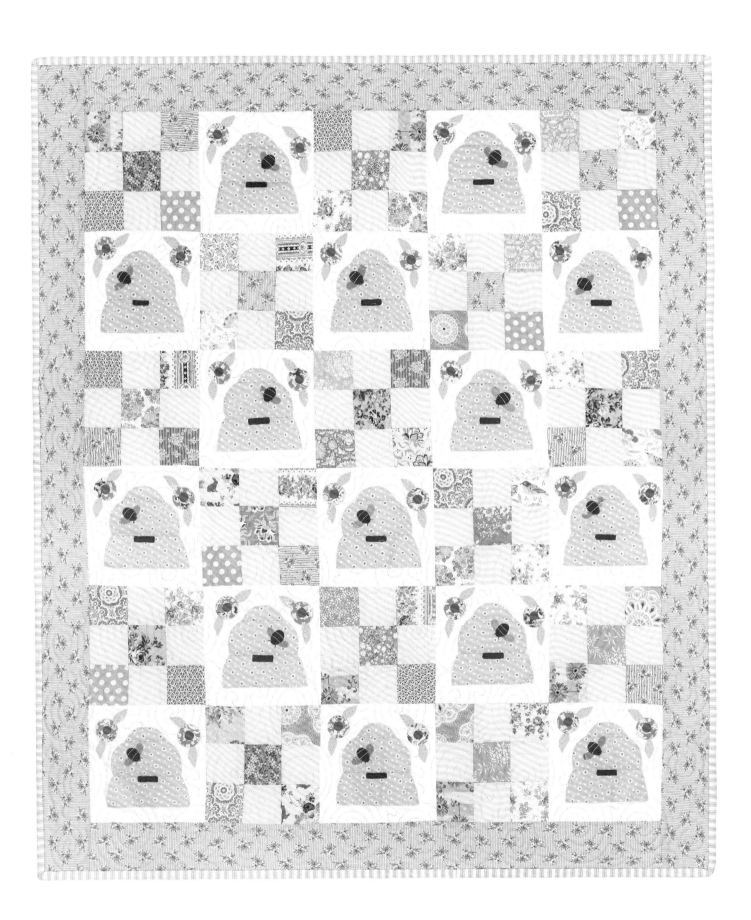

9 Draw round the large circle onto the back of the pink floral fabric twice, and draw round the small circle onto the back of the solid pink fabric twice. Draw round the leaf shape on the back of the green fabric four times.

10 Cut out the flowers and leaves and arrange as in the diagram and photo on your block. Iron in place and sew round the shapes with matching cotton.

11 This completes the beehive block.

Make fourteen more beehive blocks in the same way.

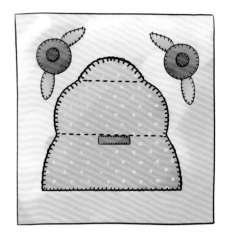

To Make the Nine Patch Block

Cut four 2 ½ in (6.35cm) squares of pale pink solid fabric and five 2 ½ in (6.35cm) squares of different printed fabrics, making sure the centre square is always a green one. Arrange the squares in rows of three and then sew together in rows with a ¼ in (6mm) seam, pressing each row in the opposite direction so the seams 'nest' neatly.

Make fourteen more nine patch blocks in the same way.

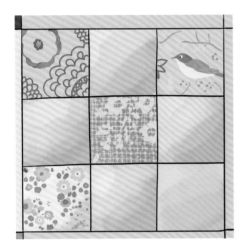

To Make Up The Quilt

To join the quilt blocks together, first lay them all out on the floor or place on a quilt wall. Check the fabrics work well in your arrangement and try not to have two fabrics the same close to each other. When you are happy with the arrangement join the blocks together in rows. Then sew the rows together, nesting the seams as before and pinning the blocks at the corners for accuracy. Press the seams.

For the Border

Cut strips of green floral fabric - two 3in x 28 1/2 in (7.62 x 72.39cm) and two 3in x 34 1/2 in (7.62 x 87.63cm)in.

For the Quilting - layer the quilt by placing the backing fabric wrong side down, place the batting on top and the quilt top facing upwards and use curved basting pins to hold all the layers together. Quilt as desired. This quilt was machine quilted with a circles pattern.

Finally bind the quilt using green striped fabric.

house & garden
SAMPLER PILLOW

This little cross stitch and patchwork pillow was inspired by the traditional house and garden samplers that I've always loved and have often stitched. The cross stitch chart is easy to follow to stitch the central panel and then the pretty fabric borders are added to the top and bottom. You could also stitch motifs from the chart onto other small items too, like greeting cards, gift tags and pincushions.

Size
10in x 10 ¼ in (25.4 x 26.04 cm) approx

YOU WILL NEED

- Pastel pink Aida fabric 12in x 6in (30.48 x 15.24cm) (trimmed to size after stitching- see below)

- DMC Stranded Cotton thread as in the key

- Size 26 tapestry needle

- 2 pieces of red floral printed fabric 10 ½ in x 3 ½ in (26.67 x 8.89cm)

- Blue ric rac 20in (51cm)

- Floral backing fabric 10 ½ in x 10 ¾ in (26.67 x 27.3cm)

- Cushion pad 10 in x 10 ¼ in (25.4 x 26.04cm)

1 Follow the chart and begin in the centre of the fabric from the centre of the chart.

2 Stitch over one block of Aida using two strands of thread for the cross stitch and one strand for the back stitch and French knots. The little grey cross stitches are also worked in one strand.

3 The trees are worked in variegated thread which gives the best effect when worked from right to left and stitching the whole stitch at a time.

4 When all the stitching is complete press the work and trim to measure 10 ½ in x 4 ½ in (26.67 x 11.43cm).

5 Cut two pieces of red floral fabric 10½ in x 3 ½ in (26.67 x 8.89cm) and sew to the top and bottom edge of the cross stitch panel. Cover the seams with blue ric rac, sewing neatly in place with matching cotton.

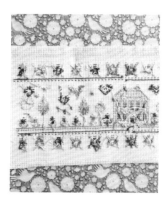

6 To make up the pillow take the backing square and place right sides together with the front, then sew round the edges leaving a gap for turning at the bottom. (You can insert a zipper here if you wish).

7 Clip the corners and turn the pillow right side out, pushing out the corners. Press the work and place the cushion pad inside, slip stitching the gap closed.

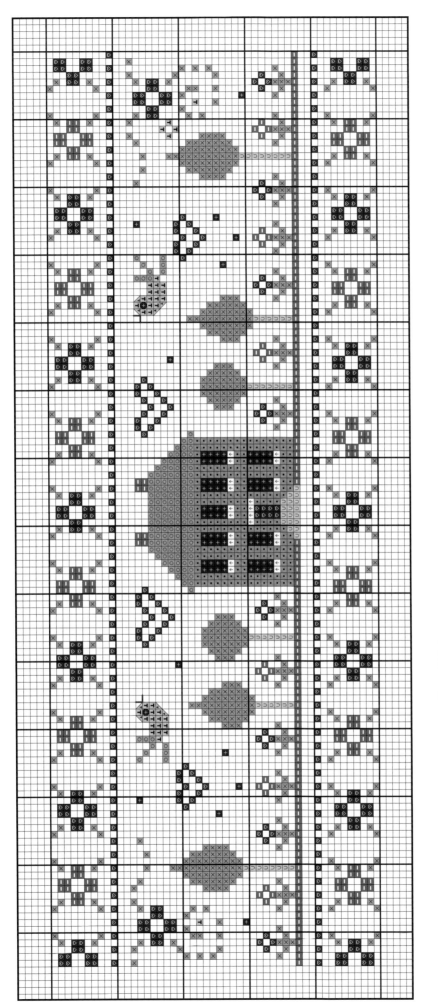

D·M·C
Mouliné
Stranded Cotton
Art. 117

Cross Stitch

3350 341 725

413 739 3326

334 Blanc

French Knot
● 413

Back Stitch
413

Half Cross Stitch
725

Color Variation
4050

liberty circles
PATCHWORK CUSHION

This cushion is the perfect way to use up those precious tiny scraps of Liberty fabric. The repeating circles and squares of solid colour fabrics make a fresh and modern design. It's a great way to enjoy those pretty little pieces of sweet traditional florals.

Size
13in x 13in (33.02 x 33.02cm) approx

YOU WILL NEED

- Pink and white striped fabric - fat quarter

- Solid blue and green fabrics in several shades

- Liberty Tana Lawn scraps

- Fusible web

- Thin card

- Solid pink fabric for borders ¼ yd (22.86cm)

- Backing fabric 13 ½ in x 13 ½ in (34.20 x 34.20cm)

- Cushion pad 13in x 13in (33.02 x 33.02cm)

1 From pink and white striped fabric cut twelve 2 ½ in (6.35cm) squares.

2 From a variety of solid blue and green fabrics cut thirteen 2 ½ in (6.35cm) squares.

3 Lay out the squares in five rows of five squares, alternating the stripes and the solids and turning the stripes the opposite way round for alternate rows.

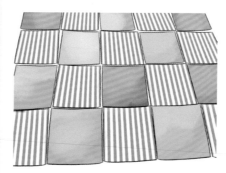

4 When you are happy with the arrangement join the squares together with a ¼ in (6mm) seam and press each row in the opposite direction so the seams nest. Then join the rows together.

5 Trace the circle template onto thin card and cut out carefully. Take 26 2in (5.08cm) scraps of Liberty fabric and iron fusible web onto the back of each one, then draw round the circle template on each one and cut them out.

6 Lay the circles in the centres of the patchwork squares on the cushion front and then remove the backing papers and iron them in place. Sew round the edge of the circles with light grey cotton and blanket stitch.

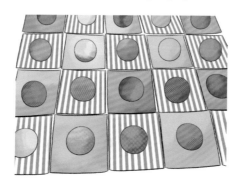

7 Cut 2 ¼ in (5.71cm) wide borders from solid pink fabric and sew to the top, bottom and sides of the cushion.

8 To make up the cushion place the backing fabric and the cushion front right sides together and sew round the sides with a ¼ in (6mm) seam leaving a gap at the bottom for turning. You can insert a zipper here if you wish. Trim the seams and clip the corners then turn the cover to the right side. Push out the corners and press.

9 Insert the cushion pad and sew the gap closed neatly.

little birds
DOLL QUILT

This pretty little doll's quilt explores patchwork, applique and embroidery in a simple and whimsical way. Children love to tuck up their toys in bed and this sweet little quilt is the perfect gift for them. This little project is jelly roll friendly, or you could use scraps from other projects to make the patchwork squares. It is such fun to make that it's tempting to make another one or even a bigger one.

Size
14 ½ x 16 ½ in (36.83 x 41.91cm) approx

YOU WILL NEED

- Various floral fabrics

- White cotton solid fabric

- Pink floral for borders

- Pale pink print for backing 16in x 18in (40.64 x 45.72cm)

- Red and white striped fabric for binding ¼ yd (22.86cm)

- Batting 16in x 18in (40.64 x 45.72cm)

- Small buttons

- Frixion pen

- Fusible web

- Red and blue embroidery thread

1 Cut 21 2 ½ in (6.35cm) squares from floral fabrics and 21 2 ½ in (6.35cm) squares from white solid cotton fabric.

2 Lay the squares out in 7 rows of 6 squares alternating floral and white squares until you are happy with the arrangement, then sew the rows together with a ¼ in (6mm) seam.

3 To make the flowers cut 12 1 ½ in (3.81cm) squares of a variety of floral fabrics and iron fusible web onto the back of each one.

4 Trace the flower shape onto thin card and cut out to make the template. Place the template on the back of the small squares and draw round, then cut it out carefully.

5 Arrange the flowers on every other row of white squares and iron in place. Sew round the flower shape with blanket stitch and matching thread.

6 Trace the bird shape and transfer to the alternate white solid cotton fabric rows, flipping the shape on alternate squares.

7 Stitch the bird using blue or red embroidery thread and split stitch. Make a French knot for the eye.

8 When the sewing and embroidery on the quilt top is complete, sew on small buttons in the centre of the flowers.

9 Cut 2 ¼ in (5.71cm) wide borders the width and length of the quilt from pink floral fabric and sew on with a ¼ in (6mm) seam.

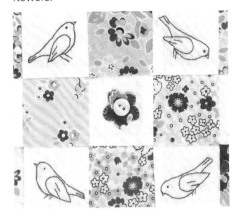

10 To make the quilt sandwich place the backing face down on a flat surface and the batting on top, then place the quilt top on that right side upwards. Pin the layers together with basting pins.

11 Quilt as desired and then bind with red and white striped binding.

little
Deer Toy

It's always fun to make a toy and simple soft fabric toys are my favourite. This little deer pattern is easy to sew using soft cotton fabric and would make a sweet gift. There are two pretty patchwork dresses to make too, perfect for using up scraps and fun to decorate with tiny buttons.

Size
12 ½ in tall (32cm) approx.

YOU WILL NEED

- Pastel solid cotton fabric 20 x 28in (50 x 70cm)

- Scraps of matching floral fabric for ear linings

- Polyester toy filling

- Black yarn

- Black beads

- Thin card

- Blusher or fabric paint

- Turning tool- optional but useful

1 Trace the deer body, arm and leg templates onto thin card and cut out.

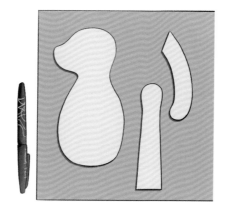

2 Fold the pastel solid cotton fabric in half and draw round the templates onto it. Do not cut out until the sewing is complete.

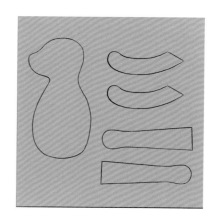

3 Sew round the body, arms and legs.

4 Trace the ear shape onto thin card and cut out. Make two ears and two ear linings by drawing round the ear shape onto pastel cotton fabric and floral fabric. Place one ear and one ear lining right sides together and sew round on the line. Repeat for the second ear. Cut out the ears and turn right side out. Gather the bottom of the ears and stitch.

5 Cut out all the shapes and turn right side out.

A turning tool is useful and quick for this part. Press the pieces and then stuff with polyester toy filling. Place the top of the legs inside the bottom of the body and stitch along the seam, catching the legs inside and backstitching at each end.

6 Stuff the arms, stitch the gap closed and sew to either side of the body. Attach the ears by sewing them to the top of the head. Or you can glue them on with fabric glue if you prefer.

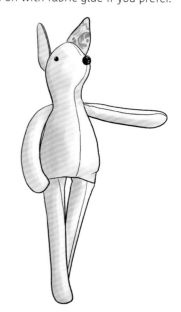

7 Make the face by sewing the nose in satin stitch with black wool and sewing on two black beads for the eyes. Add a little blusher to the cheeks if you wish.

For The Patchwork Dress

YOU WILL NEED

Patchwork Striped Dress

- 7 jellyroll strips or 2 ½ in (6.35cm) wide strips of bright contrasting fabrics

- Narrow elastic 12in (30.48cm) long

- Four tiny coloured buttons

1 Sew the 7 strips of fabric together down the long edges with a ¼ in (6mm) seam.

2 Press the work. Turn up a ¾ in (2cm) hem at the bottom edge and turn in 1in (2.5cm) down from the top. Sew in place.

3 Sew up the back seam, press and trim with pinking shears.

4 Thread the elastic through the casement at the top of the dress and pull up to fit the top of the little deer.

5 To make two straps cut floral fabric strips ¾ in (2cm) wide x 3 ½ in (8.89cm) long. Fold the sides into the middle, press and sew down the centre.

6 Attach the straps to the front and back of the dress top, crossing them over at the back. Sew on with a few small stitches. Add a tiny button at the end of each strap on the front and back.

Patchwork Squares Dress

1 Cut 18 2 ½ in (6.35cm) squares of different bright floral fabrics.

2 Sew them together in 3 rows of 6 with a ¼ in (6mm) seam.

3 When the patchwork is complete, press the work and add a 1 ½ in (3.81cm) deep band of floral fabric along the bottom. Turn a ¾ in (2cm) hem at the bottom.

4 Turn down 1in (2.5cm) from the top and stitch. Sew up the back seam and trim with pinking shears.

5 Follow steps 4 to 6 above to complete the little dress.

little

HOUSES QUILT

This little quilt is simple to sew yet it is one of my favourites because it uses pretty scraps and colourful buttons. Houses have been featured on quilts since early quilt makers used them as blocks to represent their homes. These easy applique houses can be made in any colours you choose and are fun to sew. You could also use a single applique house on other projects too, like greeting cards, pincushions or as hanging ornaments.

Size
26in x 29in (66 x 74cm) approx

YOU WILL NEED

- A variety of low volume fabrics for 30 4½ in (11.43cm) squares

- Scraps of red, blue and pink fabrics for the houses

- Fusible web

- 30 small buttons

- Thin card

- Blue gingham fabric ½ yd (45.72cm)

- Pink floral stripe for binding ¼ yd (22.86cm)

1 To make one applique house block, trace the house shape onto thin card and cut out. Iron fusible web on the back of a 2 ½ in (6.35cm) square of blue fabric and a 2 ½ x 1 ½ in (6.35 x 3.8cm) rectangle of red fabric. Draw round the house on the back of the blue fabric and round the roof shape on the red. Cut out the house and roof and iron in place on a 4 ½ in (11.43cm) low volume square, placing the roof over the top edge of the house shape. Sew round the shape with blanket stitch.

2 Cut out a door shape from red or pink fabric and iron onto the house, sewing round it with blanket stitch. Make 29 more house blocks in the same way, varying the fabrics and moving the door position to left or right on some of the houses.

3 Lay out the squares in seven rows of five squares. Join the squares together in rows with a ¼ in (6mm) seam.

4 Press each row in the opposite directions so the seams will nest together.

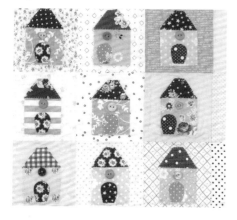

5 Sew the rows together and press the work.

6 For the border cut 4in (10.16cm) strips of blue gingham fabric the width and length of the quilt and attach with a ¼ in (6mm) seam.

7 Layer the quilt top by placing the backing fabric wrong side down on a flat surface, place the batting on top and then the quilt top facing upwards. Use curved basting pins to hold all the layers together.

8 Quilt as desired. This was machine quilted with a scribble pattern, and then hand quilting was added to the houses and little buttons were stitched on too.

9 Finally bind the quilt using a pink floral striped fabric.

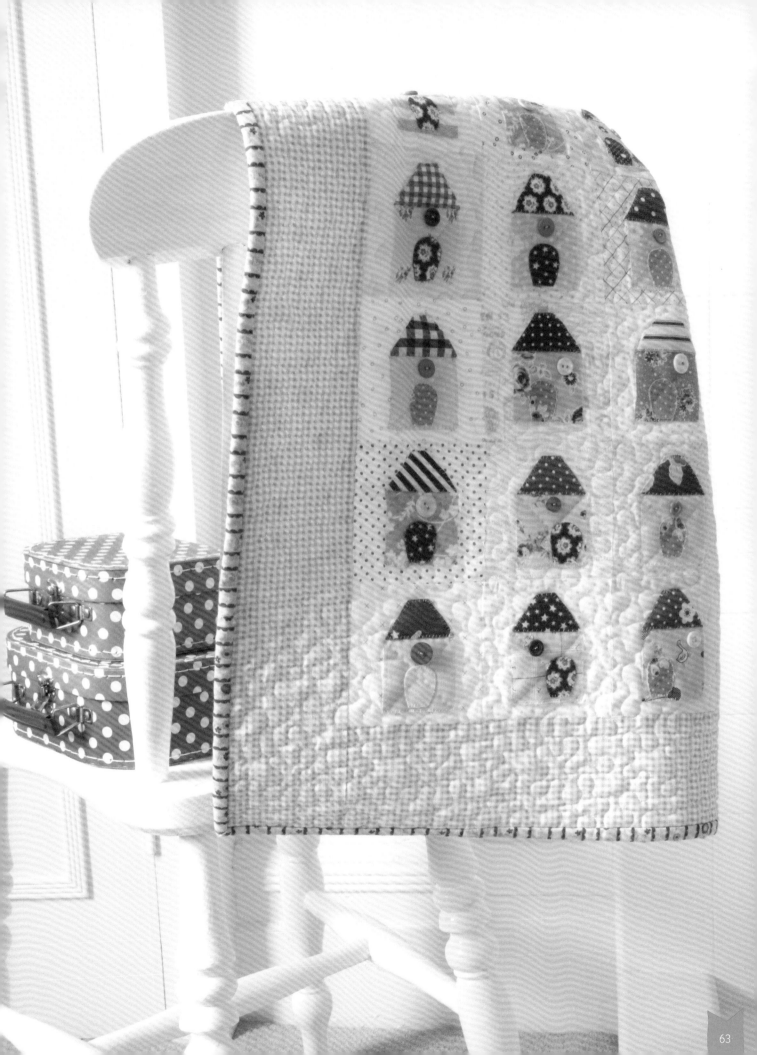

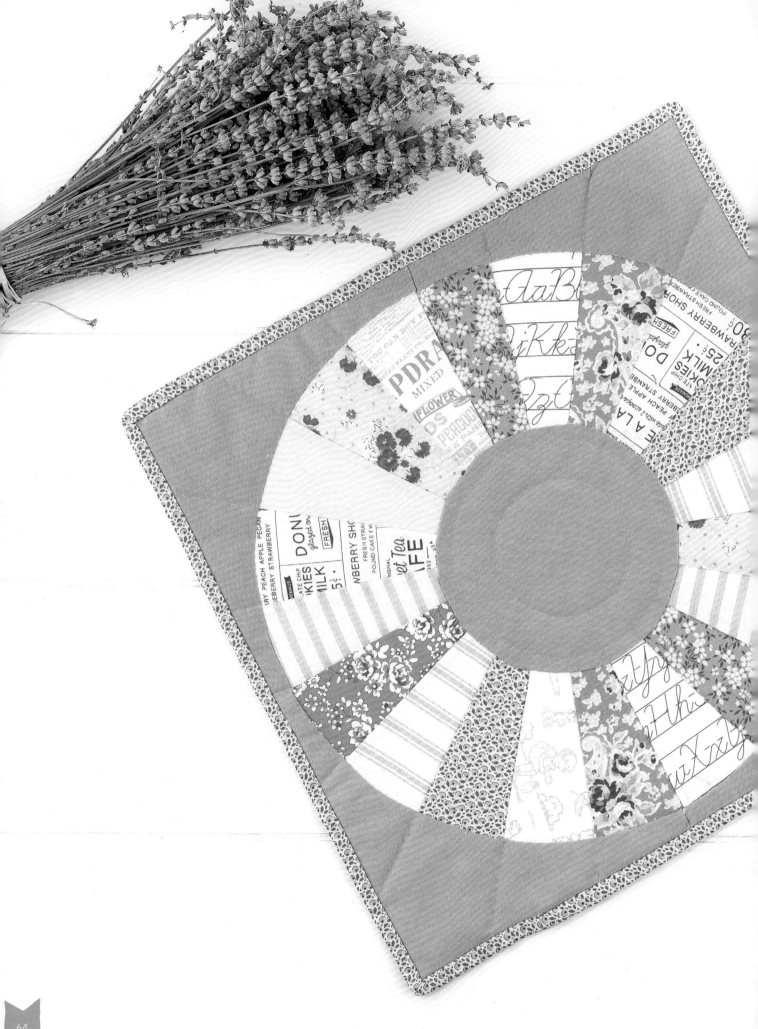

circle
TABLE TOPPER

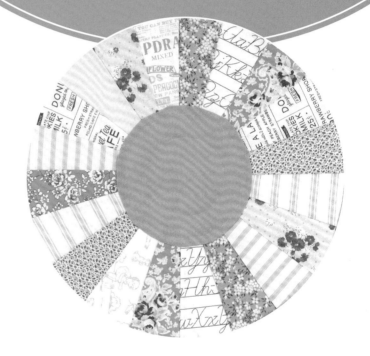

A patchwork table topper is a pretty way to bring colour and interest to a table when not in use. This pretty table topper uses soft shades of pinks and lilacs to create a decorative patchwork circle. You can also choose bright, summery colours or more festive winter ones for different times of the year. This simple patchwork project is easier to make than it looks and can be sewn by hand or by machine.

Size
13 ½ in x 13 ½ in (34.29 x 24.29) approx

YOU WILL NEED

- A variety of low volume pink and white fabrics

- Solid cotton fabric in lilac ¼ yd (22.86cm)

- Floral fabric for backing 13 ½ in x 13 ½ in (34.29 x 34.29 cm)

- Thin wadding 13 ½ in x 13 ½ in (34.29 x 34.29 cm)

- Tiny floral print fabric for binding ¼ yd (22.86cm)

- Thin card

- Frixion pen

1 Trace the templates to make the blades for the circle onto thin card and cut out.

2 Draw round the template onto the back of a piece of low volume fabric, placing the inner template on top and drawing round with a Frixion pen.

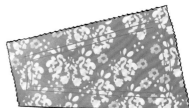

3 Cut out the blade shape along the outer line and repeat to make 20 different blades. You can repeat some of the fabrics if you wish around the circle but make sure they are not next to each other.

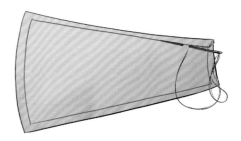

4 Sew the blades together, either by hand or machine, along the inner line on the long sides to make the circle. Press the work.

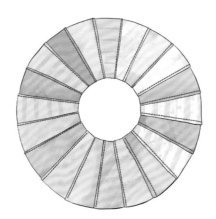
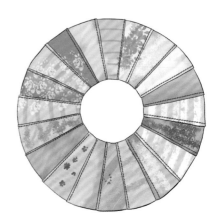

5 Cut the corner shapes from the solid lilac fabric and sew one quarter at a time to the circle, matching the seams neatly and pressing well.

6 Draw the large inner circle onto thin card and cut out carefully. Cut the large circle for the centre from solid lilac fabric, turn it inwards round the inner card circle and press. Pin in place in the middle of the patchwork circle and then needle turn applique the edges of the centre circle. Press the work well.

7 To prepare the topper for quilting, take the backing fabric and place face down on a flat surface.

8 Place the wadding on top and the patchwork on top of that facing up. Pin in place with curved basting pins. Stitch in the ditch along the blades and around the circles. Add as much or as little quilting as you wish. When the quilting is complete bind the edges of the table topper.

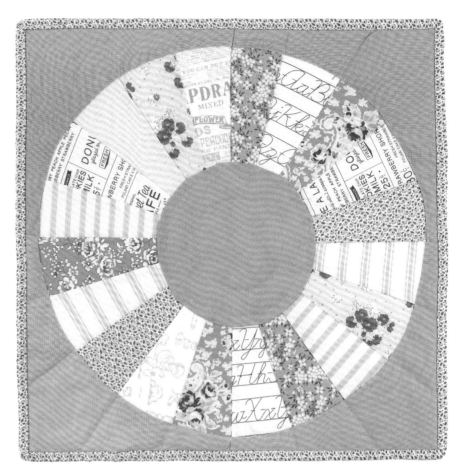

postage stamp PINCUSHION

This little project is a great way to practice English paper piecing if you haven't tried it before...and also a great project to enjoy sewing if you have! The fabrics I chose are all bright and cheery florals and I decided to add a little perching butterfly to the flowers.

Size
3 ¾ in x 3 ¾ in (9.53 x 9.53cm)

YOU WILL NEED

- Various scraps of bright fabrics for squares

- Bright fabric 4 ¼ in (11.43cm) square for backing

- Two navy floral 2 ½ in (6.4 cm) squares

- Thin card

- Scrap paper

- Green embroidery thread

- Polyester toy filling

- Glue pen

- Fusible web

1 Trace the 1in (2.5cm) square postage stamp template onto thin card and cut out.

2 Draw round the template onto scrap paper 16 times to make the squares for English paper piecing.

3 Cut out the paper squares accurately and then cut out 16 bright floral fabric squares slightly larger all round. Cover the paper squares by folding the fabric round each side and using the glue pen to secure them at the edges.

4 Lay out the squares in four rows of four until you are happy with the arrangement and then sew them together. Place the squares right sides together and over sew along the edge using tiny stitches.

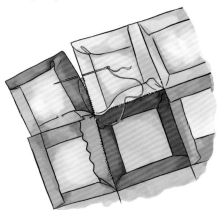

5 When the squares are all sewn together remove the papers and press. Take the backing square and with right sides together sew round the pincushion with a ¼ in (6mm) seam and leaving a small gap on one side for turning. Trim the seams and clip the corners.

6 Turn right side out and push out the corners, then press. Stuff firmly with polyester toy filling and sew up the gap.

7 To make the butterfly trace the butterfly shape onto thin card and cut out.

8 Take two 2 ½ in (6.4cm) squares of navy floral fabric and iron fusible web onto the back of one of them. Peel off the paper backing and place the two navy floral fabric squares WRONG sides together, then iron them so they fuse on the wrong side.

9 Draw round the butterfly shape on one side of the fabric square and cut out the butterfly. Press with the iron, folding the butterfly in half to form a crease down the centre.

10 Place the butterfly on the top of the pincushion and use two strands of green embroidery thread to stitch it in place. Embroider two antennae onto the pincushion at the top of the butterfly.

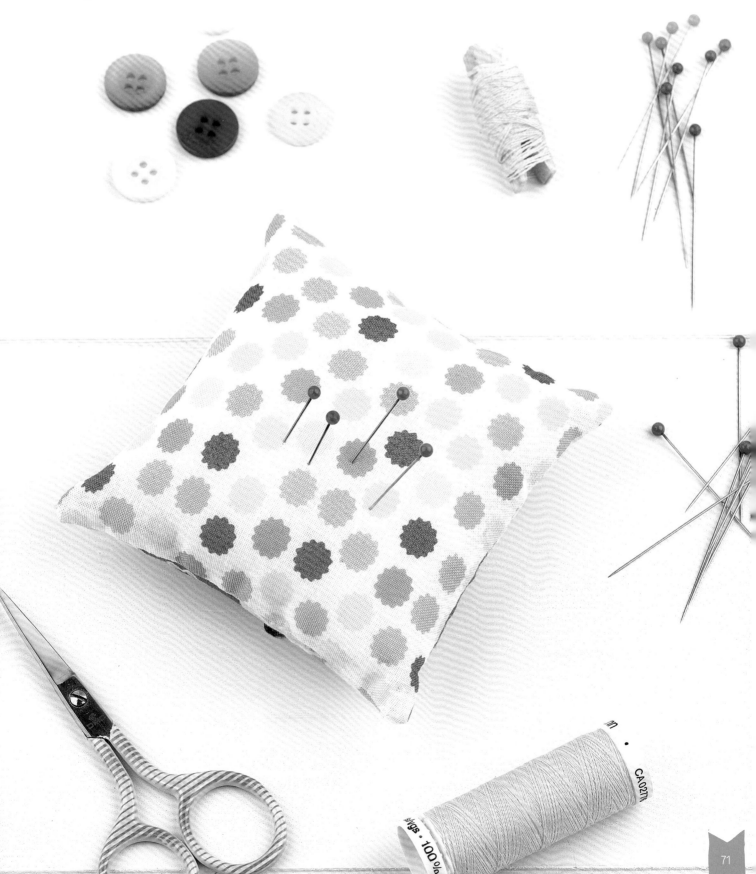

pretty patchwork DRAWSTRING BAG

This little bag is very pretty and can be used to store all kinds of things, from sewing, crochet or knitting projects to jewellery or craft tools. It would make a lovely gift especially if filled with crafty supplies or other treats. The project is easy to sew and you can have fun choosing lace, ribbon and buttons to decorate it.

Size
9 ½ in x 9in (24.13 x 22.86cm) approx

YOU WILL NEED

- Pink spot fabric
- Blue check fabric
- Scraps of different prints to make ten 2 ½ in (6.35cm) squares
- Scrap for heart applique
- Fusible web
- Red embroidery cotton
- Decorative ribbon 1yd (91.44cm)

1 To make the front of the bag cut out ten 2 ½ in (6.35cm) squares of assorted fabrics and arrange in two rows of five squares.

2 When you are happy with the arrangement sew the squares together in rows. Press the rows in opposite directions and then sew the two rows together, nesting the seams.

3 To make the heart applique iron fusible web onto the back of a 2in (5.08cm) square of blue fabric. Trace the heart shape onto the back of the fabric and cut out the heart. Place on the chosen square you wish to applique to, remove the backing from the heart and iron it in place. Stitch round the heart with matching cotton and blanket stitch. If you wish stitch a decorative line of red running stitch around the heart using embroidery thread.

4 Cut two strips of pink spot fabric 10in x 2 ½ in (25.4 x 6.35cm) and join one to the top and one to the bottom edge of the patchwork piece.

5 Cut a piece of blue check fabric 10in x 4 ½ in (25.4 x11.43cm) and sew this to the top of the bag front. Press the work.

6 To make the back of the bag cut a piece of pink spot fabric 10in x 8 ¼ in (25.4 x 20.95cm) and a piece of blue check fabric measuring 10in x 4 ½ in (25.4 x 11.43cm) and join the two pieces together along the long edges.

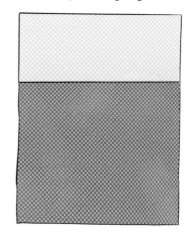

7 To make up the bag press the back and front of the bag and turn down ¼ in (6mm) at the top edge of each piece. Measure 2in (5.08cm) down from the top on each piece and mark the place with a pin at each side.

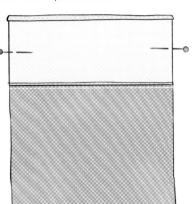

8 With right sides together sew round the whole bag from pin to pin.

9 Turn in a ¼ in (6mm) hem at the side edges of the top casement and stitch down each one close to the edge. Trim the bag seams using pinking shears to neaten.

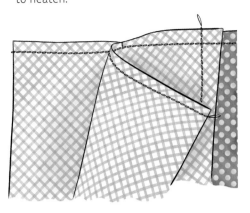

10 Fold the top edge down on the front and back and stitch in place.

11 Finally cut the ribbon into two equal lengths and thread through the casement using a safety pin. Thread one piece of ribbon in one direction and tie the ends in a knot. Thread the next piece of ribbon in the opposite direction and tie the ends in a knot. Pull up the bag to close.

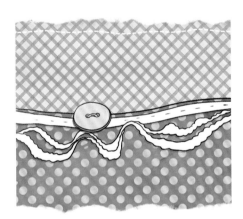

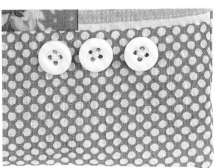

fabric CHARMS

These little charms are fun to sew and are a creative way of using up pretty fabric scraps. The charms can be used to embellish gift parcels or as a cupboard or drawer decoration, or added to a bag. Beads from old costume jewellery are perfect to add to these charms, and you could also stitch an initial or name on them.

Size
House: 2 ¼ in x 3in (5.71 x 7.62cm) approx
Heart: 2 ¼ in x 2 ¾ in (6 x 7cm) approx
Bird: 3 ¼ in x 1 ⅜ in (8.3 x 3.5cm) approx

YOU WILL NEED

- Fabric scraps

- Beads

- Polyester toy filling

- Blue and white or pink and white baker's twine

- Thin card

1 Draw round the heart shape and cut out the template.

2 Take two 3in (7.62cm) squares of floral fabric and draw round the heart template on the back of one of them. Place the two pieces of fabric right sides together and sew right round the heart shape.

3 Cut out the heart shape and make a small cut in the centre of the back for turning. Turn the heart right side out and push out the shape. Press, then stuff firmly with polyester toy filling.

4 Sew the gap closed neatly.

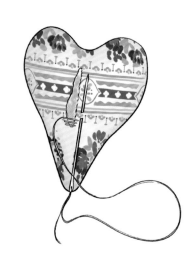

5 To decorate sew vintage style beads to the bottom of the heart and add a couple to the top centre too. Cut a 9in (22.86cm) length of blue and white baker's twine and fold in half then sew it to the top of the heart and tie in a loop to hang.

1 Trace the house shape onto thin card and cut out.

2 Take a 2 ½ in (6.35cm) square of pale floral fabric and a 1 ½ in x 2 ½ in (3.81 x 6.35cm) rectangle of red floral fabric and sew the two together with a ¼ in (6mm) seam.

3 Cut a piece of pale floral fabric 3 ½ in x 2 ½ in (8.89 x 6.35cm) for the backing.

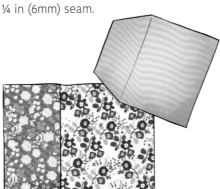

4 Place the front and back pieces right sides together and place the house template on the back of the front piece, aligning the roof edge with the seam. Draw round with a washable pen. Pin and sew round the house shape leaving a gap at the bottom for turning.

5 Turn the house shape the right way out and push out the corners. Stuff with polyester toy filling. Applique a small rectangle to the front to make a door.

6 Take a 20in (50 cm) length of pink and white baker's twine and tie a knot in the bottom. Choose beads to match the fabric colours and thread three onto the baker's twine, then tie and knot and push the needle up through the house and out at the top. Thread on a small bead here. Take the thread out of the needle and tie in a knot to form a loop.

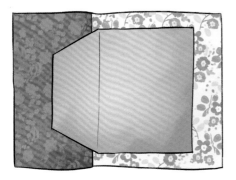

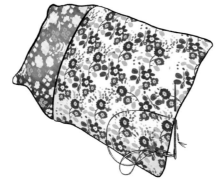

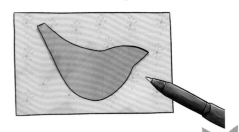

Bird Charm

1 Trace the bird shape onto thin card and cut out to make a template.

2 Take two rectangles of fabric 4in x 2 ½ in (10.16 x 6.35cm) and place them right sides together.

3 Draw round the bird template on the back of one piece of fabric, then sew round the shape leaving a gap where marked for turning.

4 Cut out the bird shape and turn right side out.

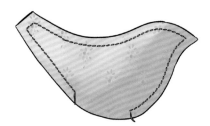

5 Push out the shape carefully, especially the beak and the tail.

6 Stuff with polyester toy filling and sew up the gap.

7 Thread a 20in (50cm) long piece of pink and white baker's twine with three beads to match the bird fabric and push the needle through the bird and out at the top. Add another bead here, then remove the needle and tie the twine in a knot to form a loop.

spring time WREATH

Making a fabric wreath is fun and a creative way to use up scraps of fabric, felt and even tiny purchased or found seasonal decorations. This little wreath brings a breath of spring with its fresh colours, fabric flowers, leaves, butterfly and speckled eggs. You can keep it simple or add as many embellishments as you like. The fabric flower and butterfly are sweet little makes to add to other projects too, like pincushions and bags.

Size
6 ¾ in x 6 ¾ in (17 x 17cm) approx

YOU WILL NEED

- Polystyrene wreath 170 mm
- Pale blue check cotton fabric
- Pink cotton fabric
- Green floral fabric
- Green felt
- Scraps of white felt
- Covered buttons
- Polystyrene speckled eggs
- Raffia
- Glue gun or strong glue
- Tiny yellow paper flowers
- Scraps of blue and pink fabric
- Pink gems
- Fusible web
- Frixion pen

1 To cover the polystyrene wreath cut 2 ½ in (6.4cm) strips of blue check fabric and join with a ¼ in (6mm) seam until you have a 90in (228.6cm) length.

2 Fold in half along the length and iron the crease. Roll into a ball and then pin one end to the back of the polystyrene wreath and wind the remainder round the wreath until it is covered.

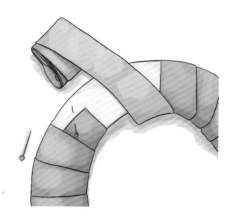

3 Secure the end at the back with pins.

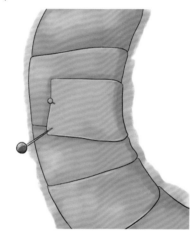

To Make the Pink Fabric Flowers

1 Trace the circle template onto thin card and cut out carefully.

2 Place the circle onto the back of the pink fabric and draw round it five times to make five petals.

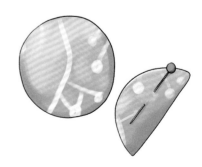

3 Fold one circle in half and sew round the raw edge with white cotton and running stitch, pulling it up to gather. Go straight on to the next petal in the same way. When all five petals are joined pull the thread to gather them all up, place the first and last petals together and overstitch to finish. Glue a small circle of white felt onto the back of the flower to secure the petals.

 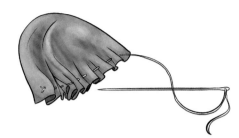 

4 To make a covered button you will need a circle of green floral fabric and a button shell. Sew a line of running stitch round the outside of the circle and pull up round the button shell. Over sew at the back to secure. Push the round button back into place to finish. Glue the covered button to the centre of the pink flower with a glue gun or strong glue.

5 Make another two pink flowers in the same way.

6 Trace the leaf shape onto thin card and use it to cut seven leaves from green felt.

To Make the Butterfly

1 Trace the butterfly shape onto thin card and cut out.

3 Draw round the butterfly shape on the pink fabric with Frixion pen and cut out the shape. Press with the iron, forming a crease down the centre of the butterfly. Thread a needle with two strands of grey embroidery cotton and back stitch along the centre line.

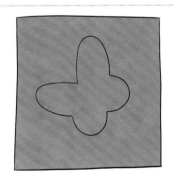

2 Take a 2 ½ in (6.4cm) square of pink and a 2 ½ in (6.4cm) square of blue fabric and iron fusible web onto the back of one of them. Place the two pieces of fabric WRONG sides together, removing the paper backing, and bond them together with the iron.

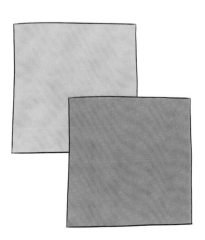

4 Glue two pink gems to the back of the wings.

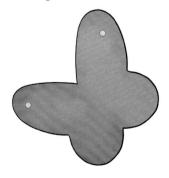

1 Arrange the pink flowers with leaves behind them on the front of the wreath. When you are happy with the arrangement glue each element in place with a glue gun.

2 Cut some little pieces of raffia and arrange between the flowers with a speckled egg on top.

3 Add some little yellow paper flowers here and there and perch the butterfly, gluing it along the centre but leaving the wings free.

4 Finally pin a piece of twine or ribbon to the back to hang.

TEMPLATES

Circle Table Topper

Page 64

Outer Line = Cutting Line

Inner Line = Fold Line For Needleturn Applique

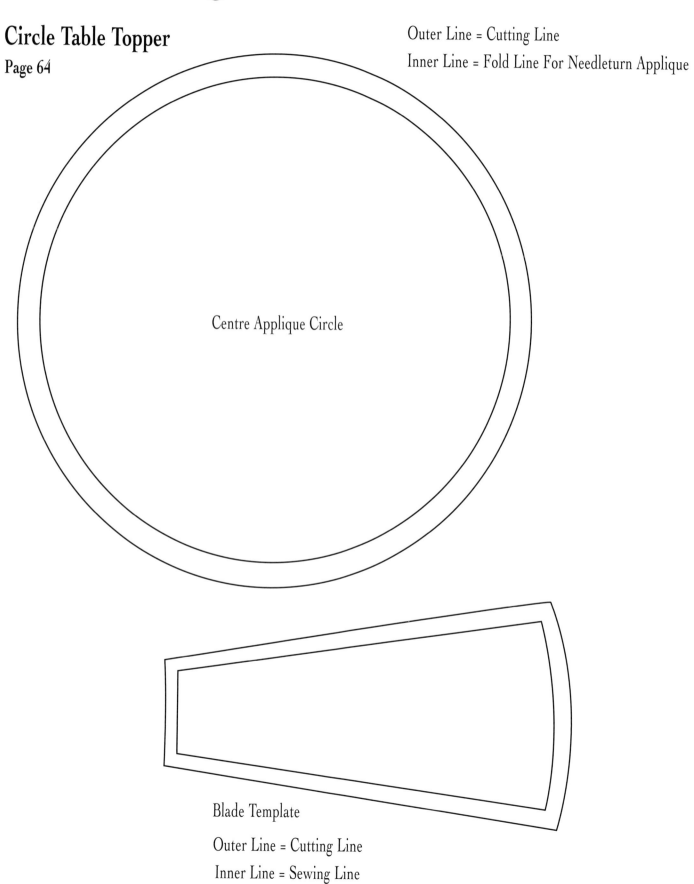

Centre Applique Circle

Blade Template

Outer Line = Cutting Line

Inner Line = Sewing Line

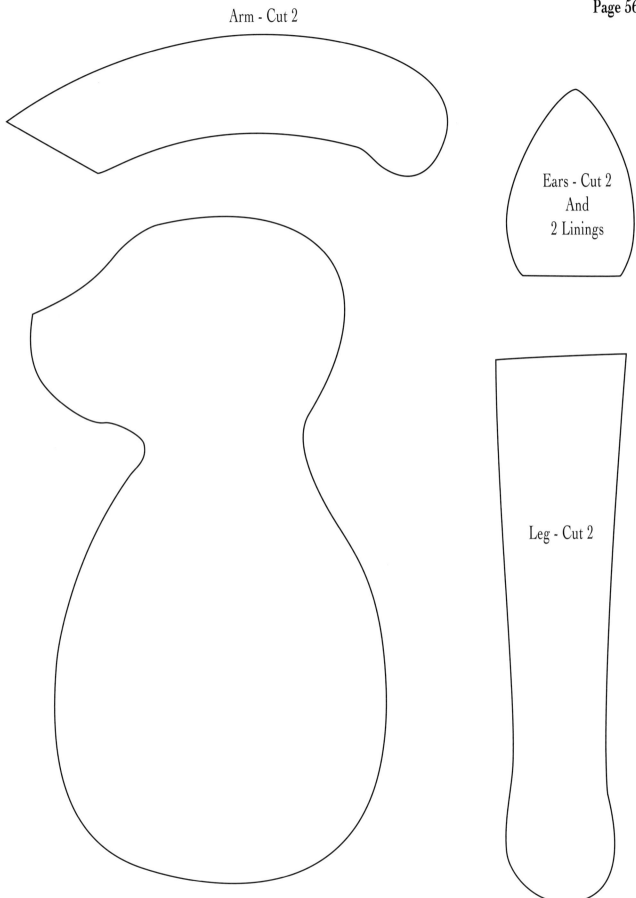

Arm - Cut 2

Ears - Cut 2
And
2 Linings

Leg - Cut 2

Arm - Cut 2

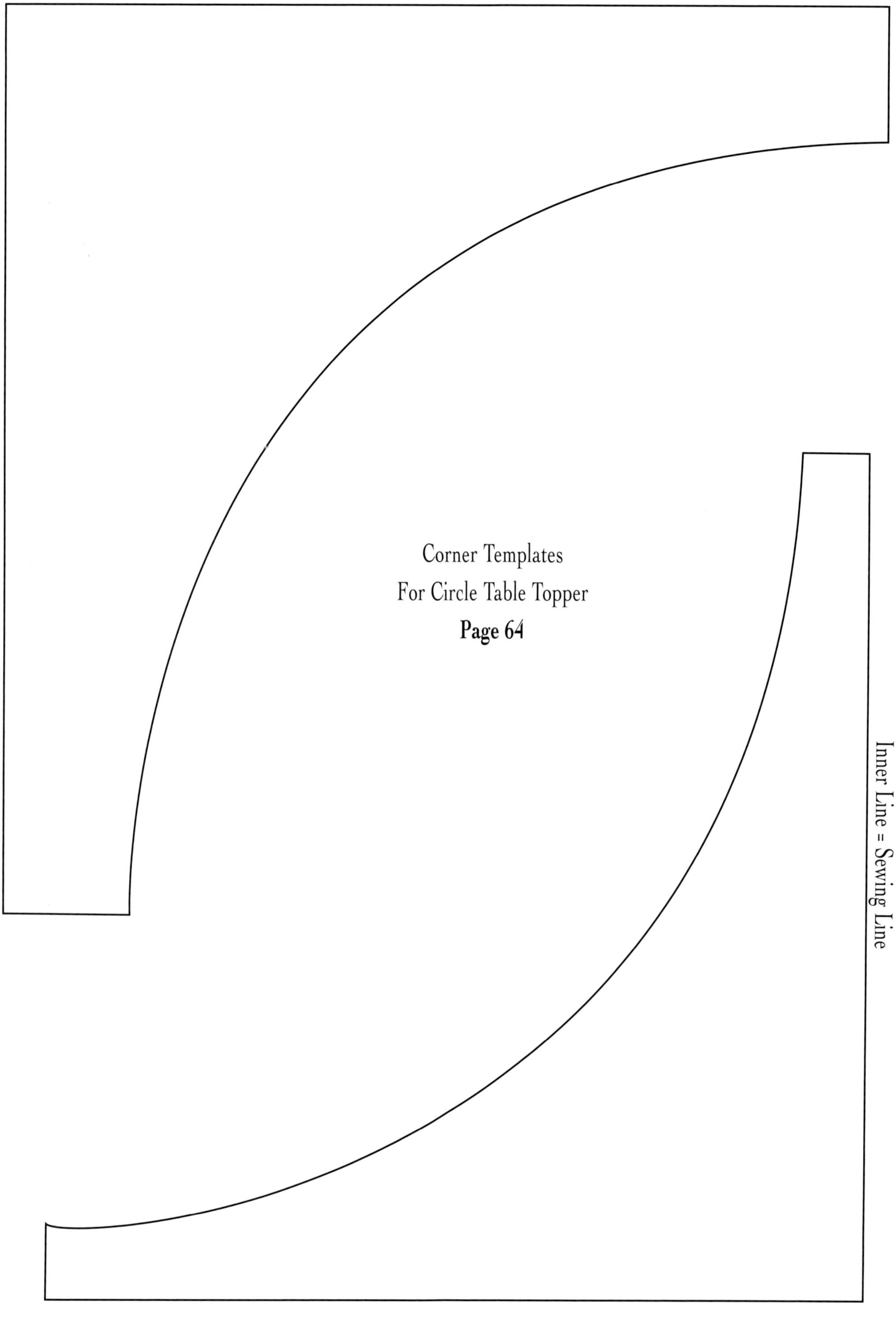

Corner Templates
For Circle Table Topper
Page 64

Liberty Circles Pillow
Page 48

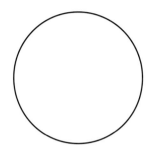

Heart Charm

House Charm

Bird Charm

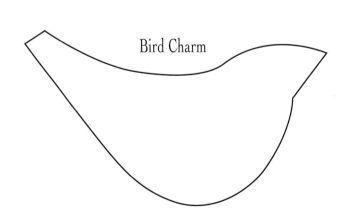

Honey Hives Quilt
Page 38

Bee Body
Bee Wing

Beehive

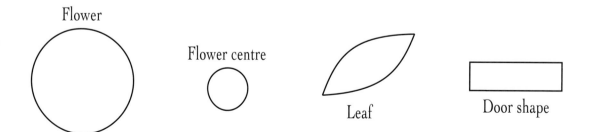

Flower

Flower centre

Leaf

Door shape

Pretty Patchwork
Drawstring Bag
Page 72

Heart applique

Page 24
Flower Cone

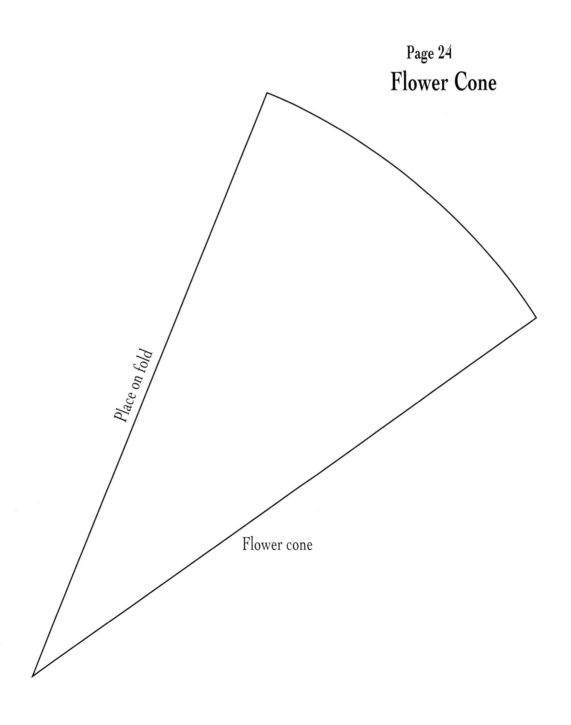

Place on fold

Flower cone

Spring Time Wreath
Page 82

Leaf

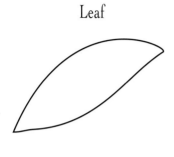

Flower Petal
(used for Flower Bag too)

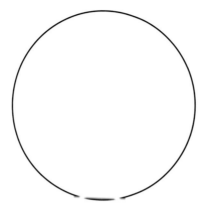

Butterfly
(also Postage Stamp pincushion)

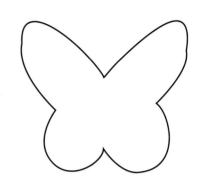

Hexagon Flower Coaster
Page 34

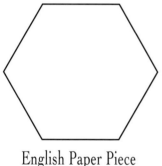

English Paper Piece
Hexagon

Cherry Zipper Pouch
Page 10

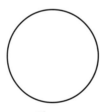

Cherry

Leaf

Little Birds Doll Quilt
Page 52

Bird embroidery

Applique flower

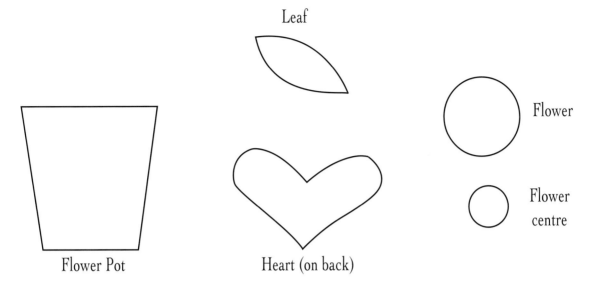

Leaf

Flower

Flower
centre

Flower Pot

Heart (on back)

Little Houses Quilt

Page 60

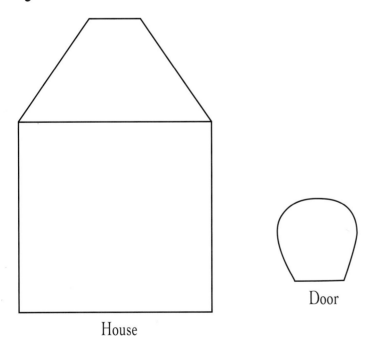

House

Door

Dresden Pincushion

Page 14

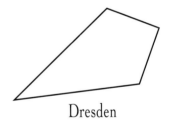

Dresden